# THE ART
# OF DISCOVERY

*Fueling Innovation
for Company Growth*

# THE ART
# OF DISCOVERY

*Fueling Innovation
for Company Growth*

WAYNE M. BUNDY, PH.D.

CRISP PUBLICATIONS

Editor-in-Chief: *William F. Christopher*

Managing Editor: *Kathleen Barcos*

Editor: *Amy Marks*

Cover Design: *Kathleen Barcos*

Cover Production: *Russell Leong Design*

Book Design & Production: *London Road Design*

Printer: *Bawden Printing*

**Library of Congress Card Catalog Number 97-65793**

**ISBN 1-56052-438-3**

# CONTENTS

# PREFACE

I write this book from the view of thirty-four years of experience as a technology leader. During this time I learned the great importance of designing discovery approaches that go beyond the scientific method. It should not come as a great surprise that little has been written about how to achieve discovery in science and technology. Without a clear path that will ensure success, discovery arises in the most varied of ways. Many kinds of people create, and their ways cannot be reduced to a clear, predictable pattern. The way the brain leads the creator to the novel is largely unknown; the whole picture is in the realm of chaos. On the plus side, a great deal of knowledge points to those actions and environments that promote creativity and ease discovery.

In recent years, social scientists have learned much about the nature of creativity. Neuroscientists have made strides in their knowledge of how the brain functions. Some common personal traits and some kinds of actions have been identified that can be helpful to the creative firm. Using these sources of knowledge and calling upon my own background, I have designed guidelines for discovery. During my career, I have used many of the actions outlined in this book with success.

I contend that aesthetics is a major aspect of discovery. It instills the will to discover. Without intense joy in the search, I suppose that discoveries still could be made, if only by the plodding use of scientific method and serendipity. It is my belief, though, that aesthetics is the prime driving force of the greatest findings. Ranging from satisfaction to rapture, this feeling of discovery can be awe, beauty, and joy, or even strangeness.

If you feel a hunger for breadth in knowledge, if you thrive on the tension created by varied beliefs, if you feel the great need to resolve such tension, if you are moved by a profound desire to approach truth, and if you are inclined toward iconoclasm, you must be a revolutionary scientist. If not, you are one in spirit. The appeal of novel ideas can be realized fully in actual settings only. In these settings, the spirit that discovery brings can be highly contagious.

After having worked as a scientist for the New Mexico Bureau of Mines and the Indiana Geological Survey, and then earning my Ph.D. from Indiana University, I went into industry. This move from academe and pure science to industry and applied science seemed at first to be a major movement away from intellectual work. What quickly became clear, however, is that a closeness exists between science and technology, a symbiosis, which helps both grow to higher levels. This link between pure science and pure technology must be managed with care to encourage novel advances and successful innovation.

Sometimes, novel advances are made in firms without the aid of research. Most major advances in technology, however, could not occur without this quest for new knowledge. Such advances often arise from the leading edge of science. Basic research in each leading area, geared toward strategic company goals, is needed most of the time to promote the creation of novel ideas.

Conflicts often exist between the methods of business and technology management. To do good work one must be aware of these conflicts. If a major company goal is innovation, the most important knowledge to have is an understanding of how to achieve discovery. If innovation is your primary goal and is crucial to your ego and career, it must be pursued no matter what stands in the way. Therein reside the major aims of this book: to advance your knowledge of how to achieve discovery, to give new vigor to your long-term efforts, and above all, to help you realize your full potential.

One more important goal is to help business leaders promote innovation through basic knowledge of the discovery process. Such knowledge should greatly relieve the tension that often exists between technologists and business leaders, and enhance both the process of gaining novel ideas and of changing them into profit.

# I.

# A NEW MODEL FOR CREATIVITY

T HIS BOOK PRESENTS A NEW model for creativity, shown in Figure 1. This model adds two stages to the classic model: knowledge gain prior to preparation, and stimulation coactive with incubation. Creativity will not happen without knowledge gain, which is the first stage in the model.

## Knowledge Gain

Through gaining knowledge about a subject, we arouse our own interest in that subject. In other words, the more ways we can address a problem, the more interest we can accrue. It is impossible to know a subject well unless it has been viewed from many angles. Knowledge growth is essential in order to nurture the intellect. Equally important, it helps build the desire that fuels our drive. Without drive, discovery would be achieved rarely.

Edward de Bono cautioned about the dangers of too much knowledge to novel thinking.[1] It can promote mind-sets and preclude serendipity. This danger does exist, if one has worked many years within one paradigm.

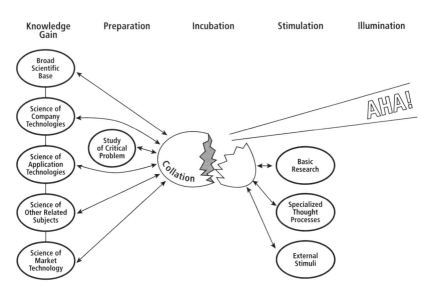

*Figure 1.   A schematic for industrial creativity*

Although escape from this trap is never easy, three approaches may be helpful.

The first approach is to conduct diverse research, which helps one to maintain a broader view of nature. From this diversity, one gets a wide range of knowledge that precludes minute detail and requires the insight to fix in mind the critical points.

The second approach is to remind oneself of the dynamic and uncertain nature of knowledge. Aware of uncertainty, one is more likely to maintain an open approach to problems. The third approach is to seek other ideas that may provide a more useful perspective. If knowledge is stored as rigid systems, creativity is not favored. If it is stored in broad classes for ready association, much knowledge can only aid the process. To be confined to one concept is the curse of those who wish to create. Those who create use their stores of knowledge for discovery.

Discoveries are made by those who have a unique blend of knowledge, theories, and models. To address this core need of creativity, all of the knowledge patterns in one's field of study should be researched often. Even doing research in areas of science related but largely outside the scope of one's field can be helpful. Efforts should be made to relate varied patterns of knowledge in the hopes of coming up with a useful new idea. The English scientist Michael Faraday was most adept at seeing value in the blend of diverse knowledge. He showed the connection between electricity and magnetism and their relation to light, and how electricity is involved in the building of matter.

In industry, research most often relates to company goals, which can be called directed basic research. Unlimited time between new products is not a privilege of the business world. Basic work that does not lead directly to new products (nondirected basic research), therefore, often should be handled by outside labs. Both types of basic research are crucial. At least half of all inventions stem from nondirected basic research.[2]

Some people in industry argue that basic research, if really needed, should be consigned to outside labs in order to allow companies to spend more time on current problems. Often this action may be the only valid approach; however, companies should conduct as much basic research in-house as possible. Those who do research gain an insight that cannot be transferred fully to others. It is this subtle knowledge that can lead to superb new product teams.

David Bloor describes another view of knowledge.[3] He says that knowledge is not just a mirror image of nature that any person can gain. It is the product of the interaction of our knowledge and our culture with a new experience. Such an effect can be viewed by way of the parallelogram of forces (see Figure 2). Each person and each culture provides a unique response to new events, which accounts for highly varied points of view.

This view of knowledge explains many of the conflicts in ideas. On the plus side, the wealth of notions offered is crucial. Just as there are many valid ways to study events that are crucial to knowledge, there are many concepts that when interacted can lead to novel ideas.

Much evidence exists that intelligence is not fixed— that it can be increased through guided learning. People who adjust to new environments are using a process for

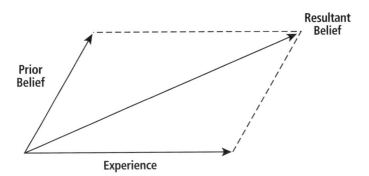

*Figure 2.   Parallelogram of forces showing that prior belief and experience influence resultant belief*

growing intelligence. In the past 2.5 million years, many abrupt climatic changes have resulted in major changes in life. For example, during this time our brains enlarged to their present size.[4] In concert with Darwin's concept of evolution, brain growth was a chance event that addressed a need. Drastic change in environment is one of many plausible explanations of cause.

Gerald Edelman saw the brain as the most complex object in nature.[5] The brain is always changing, and the more challenging the environment, the better the change. Having between $10^{12}$ and $10^{14}$ nerve cells, the brain's neuron cables linking these cells are several kilometers in length within one cubic millimeter of cerebral cortex.[6] New concepts that could come from these nerve cell contacts should be countless. The recent concept that mental exercise can change the brain should have a large influence on what we can do to enhance our problem-solving talent.

Some experts believe that learning leads to new synaptic linkages.[7] Synapses are gaps between nerve cells. Contact across gaps occurs via chemicals known as neurotransmitters. Neuron and chemical change in brain structure is called plasticity. Varying among animals, plasticity is limited in insects and strong in human beings.[8] Among humans, it is strongest with children but still exists in adults. Thus every experience effects brain change. Learning is a way of changing our brain's structure for enhanced thinking.

Research, where it involves a broad range of projects, provides a major basis for exploiting our brain's plasticity. Knowledge gain in these areas must be coupled with a constant effort to relate the obvious and the odd. Such a method can reveal new concepts that can knead and reshape the intellect.

If people are to create new products in the best way, they must learn their customer's cultures and systems. Living with customers to some degree is the only way of gaining a clear grasp of their new product needs. It is through such knowledge that the best new product efforts can be carried out in the lab. Customers have unique problems that cannot be grasped without inside knowledge. Lab work alone is not enough. Without a profound knowledge of market needs, new product efforts probably will not succeed.

The nature of needed knowledge is often outside the scope of traditional market research. Such work can be carried out best by the people involved in the new product program. To aid on-site knowledge, these same people should have close market contacts. This way, the technologists can begin to sense or intuit the most important aspects of customer needs. From personal contact, the technologists may develop insight into the crucial requirements for a new product. The market knowledge needed includes:

1.  Determine customer's use of your product.

2.  Determine nature and function of all system parts. Combine this data with costs.

3.  Research relevant literature.

4.  Interpret data.

5. Project new product needs and how your knowledge might be focused to address these needs.

To address a core need of creativity, one must research the knowledge patterns shown in Figure 3 (see also Figure 1). But the question almost always arises: How can one find the time to do all of this research? Because pressing current problems take the lead, the usual answer

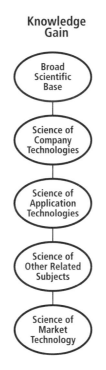

*Figure 3.* **Knowledge essential to technological creativity**

is that the time *cannot* be found. The solution to this problem is not simple: It requires a clear administrative grasp of the needs of research and a strong drive by the technical people.

To expand creative capabilities, there must be an intense drive for knowledge and a clear desire to do all of the projects chosen. Also, projects should be viewed in the sense of pleasure—never as chores, never done with an eye toward monetary reward. Creativity requires full commitment. If this simple notion were fully grasped and carried out, profit should skyrocket. Research labs must have the passion to persist in knowledge gain.

The strongest drive of many researchers is the subtle yet profound stimulation that stems from knowledge growth. After much research, Albert Rothenberg found that motivation is the only trait common to all creative people.[9] Those who have found their talent to discover new knowledge have an aura of enthusiasm. Such zeal is infectious. Even those who are not inventors are apt to be caught up in the enthusiasm. Technical people with this syndrome are happy with their work. People who have the drive must be allowed to do research, to theorize, and to invent. Without this opportunity, the firm will lose a major source of wealth—motivated people!

The first step in the creative process, knowledge gain, must persist where discovery is the goal. It leads to the solving of many problems and is useful for preparation, the next step in the model for creativity. Socrates believed that the greatest cause of evil is ignorance. Knowledge was the touchstone of ancient Greek thought,[10] as it is for all who create.

# Preparation

Knowledge gain is general; preparation is specific. A complex problem must be approached from every angle with intense thought. It is helpful to management and to technologists to know how problem solving will advance business goals.

If one has a choice of the problem to pursue, that choice should be made with care. Most people work on routine problems and follow conventional guidelines. It is not easy to create novel concepts by working on fad problems. One must search for those problems that have been overlooked and that are anomalies. Often, problems are shunned because they are complex or because they are not vogue, yet the greatest chance to excel and to make breakthroughs is in these areas.

A preferred way to approach a new problem is to create an algorithm. As once observed, the trouble with life is that you're half way through before you realize that it's one of those things that you must do yourself. Algorithms enable researchers to touch all the bases and to stretch the mind. They do not, however, ensure discovery. In my early research career, my programs were not as well conceived as I would have liked. Even worse, I was tied too closely to the logical empiricism of science. I often wondered if an algorithm, formal or informal, could be devised that would enhance chances of success. A mathematical formula, such as Newton's for gravitational attraction, is formal and useful to only a narrow aspect of nature. The scientific method is informal and a potent method useful to the whole of science.

Using a principle like the scientific method, I designed an approach to problem solving that included actions likely to arouse novel ideas. To improve chances for creativity, a process of science should include the following:

1. methods for the constant growth of knowledge and broad interaction

2. a variety of thought methods

3. a holistic approach, whenever possible

Growth of knowledge comes through a broad range of literature and lab research and through an exchange of ideas with peers. It is not the gaining of knowledge per se that leads to new ideas but rather the interaction of varied research, knowledge patterns, and unique ways of thinking (see Figure 4). It is like the moiré phenomenon, where the blending of sounds of two or more rhythmic patterns can produce a third coherent pattern or sound. For example, two very high frequency patterns can be combined in a way that produces a low frequency sound heard by the human ear. This newly formed sound typifies the nonlinearity of nature and novel concepts.

To increase chances for the most fruitful knowledge blend, the broadest range of thought must be used. Helpful methods include exchange both in-house and among global contacts, concept and problem-solving sessions, and novel thought processes (see Chapter II). Futile efforts by people when they are pressed for world-class ideas stem largely from a lack of a knowledge base and a system that fails to promote knowledge interaction.

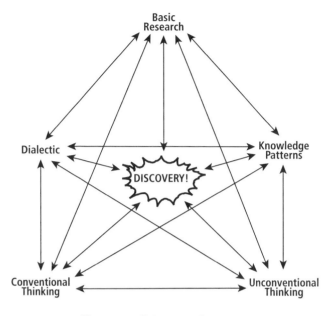

*Figure 4. Discovery thrives in a
highly interactive environment*

Concept and problem-solving sessions can take many
forms, such as brainstorming, synectics, think-tank systems,[11] and skunk works.[12] Any of these methods can be a
good tool if led by strong and knowing leaders who follow
through. Leadership must include openness, suspension of
judgment, and strong efforts to make new ideas function
as problem-solving methods. New concepts are often the
offspring of big egos, which must be treated with tender,
loving care to maintain the flow of ideas. For the most useful ideas to be found, participants must have knowledge of
all company functions and needs.

A firm that strongly supports technology promotes creativity and new ideas. In stark contrast, the waxing and waning of support is harmful to the novel spirit. The base for new ideas builds on a complex of knowledge interaction over many years. Unless a company is willing to support long-term knowledge gain projects on a continuing basis, its return on research dollars is likely to be small.

Holistic thinking involves the combined action of two or more knowledge patterns. In other words, a variety of knowledge patterns must be integrated if discovery is to occur. For example, in a kaolin study (a clay mineral widely used in manufacturing), a single aspect of kaolin (e.g., base-exchange) could be studied. But a more holistic approach would involve study of several aspects of kaolin, such as the combined action of the surface chemistry and surface physics; structural, optical, and compositional properties; particle geometry; application areas; and rheological properties.

Discovered kaolin knowledge should be interacted not only with information already known, but with plant needs for making the product, the nature of the crude material, market needs, and costs. The person discovering new knowledge should study all of these things, and their potential effect on profit as well. This approach is necessary for three reasons: (a) to ensure follow-through in finding and making known the likely profit, (b) to understand the limits of a concept and, therefore, how to approach problems with more insight and, (c) to react with the widest possible range of knowledge patterns. This threefold approach increases chances for the creation of novel ideas. The algorithm should accomplish the following goals:

1. Defining the problem: nature and opportunities

2. Assembling the key in-house knowledge about the problem

3. Ranking the research needed to enhance problem solving

4. Deriving direct ways to solve the problem

5. Provide interaction of the research group's knowledge and wisdom

These objectives form the basis of the algorithm shown in Table 1.

When answers to research questions are not known or cannot be found in the literature, a clear need exists for carrying out research. Conducting targeted research without the basic science is a common source of wasted money. When research questions are answered, however, the framework for a new product has been derived. The targeted research, then, becomes a direct target. Problems are often solved satisfactorily and then stopped. However, creative people search constantly for a better way to do things. Routine answers to problems can be easy, but the novel and most useful answers take great effort.

If the original goal is not achieved, the result should not be called failure. In science and technology, failure occurs only if the effort is lacking. If the question is not answered, despite a noble effort, a great amount has been learned. This new knowledge not only provides a needed background for solving other problems but may lead to a solution to the first problem.

| Who | Actions |
|---|---|
| Individual | • Give a clear and concise definition of the problem. |
| | • List all useful goals. |
| | • In one or two statements, show key knowledge about the problem. Search for false beliefs. |
| | • List the basic knowledge you believe should be known to solve the problem. Highlight needed research. |
| | • Rank research goals. |
| | • Show how materials might be changed to address the problem. |
| | • List proposed problem-solving methods. |
| Group | • Discuss best methods after individual presentations have been made. |
| | • Review research results for group learning and to determine changes needed for improved approach. |
| Individual and Group | • As new knowledge is found, search for possible ways to apply the knowledge. |
| | • Look for a range of ways to analyze the data. |
| | • Think about the impact on the whole of knowledge and, if useful, show costs. |

*Table 1.   An algorithmic approach to problem solving*

## Incubation

Often, preparation does not lead to problem solving. But incubation, the next stage in the creativity model, may be the best route to the creation of novel ideas. A shaky concept, incubation is a process that may take place in the nonconscious mind. It may take over when conscious thought is no longer helpful. The nonconscious may be a source of novel concepts (see Figure 5).

The brain stores knowledge at many levels, not all of which can be accessed by the conscious mind. This scheme can explain intuition, hunches, and the like. It can explain our nonconscious minds as well. Each of us, by this account, is far more knowing than our conscious mind allows us to display at any given time. Sometimes leading to new things, new knowledge may interact with a vast storehouse of knowledge in our nonconscious minds.

*Figure 5. Nonconscious thought may be important to novel ideas*

## Conscious versus Nonconscious Thinking

The relation of conscious and nonconscious thinking is shown by Figure 6 and was modified after a diagram obtained from Chuck House.[13] For example, in early life we are not aware that we do not know how to tie our shoes (see lower right portion of the figure). This is the first stage of incompetency and is nonconscious. Next, we learn that we do not know how to tie our shoes, which is the last part of the incompetent stage and is conscious. After we learn how to tie our shoes, we have reached the conscious stage of knowing that we know. At the last stage of competency, tying our shoes has become a habit, and

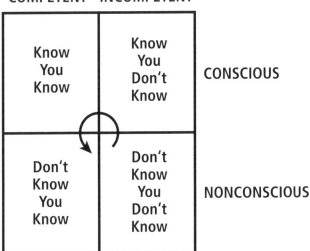

**COMPETENT  INCOMPETENT**

| Know You Know | Know You Don't Know | CONSCIOUS |
| Don't Know You Know | Don't Know You Don't Know | NONCONSCIOUS |

*Figure 6. Problem solving via the conscious and the nonconscious*

we carry out the act without overt thinking (nonconscious stage of competency).

A basic problem of doing novel things is that it requires the talent to move from habit to the knowledge of incompetence. It is a problem of moving at will back and forth when we must gain new competencies. We must learn to use our conscious minds to overcome mind-sets and habits that block our growth in knowing. Growth in science requires that we change our patterns of knowledge. Being a process that is contrary to human nature, change in thought for stubborn problems must become a common method for those who wish to create.

Freud believed that dreams are mirrors of our unconscious minds. People who study dreams today believe that the mind is never dormant or unconscious and that mental action occurs even in the deepest sleep. In the dream state of sleep, mental action is close to that of the awake state. The free imagery of dreaming and the frequent offbeat thoughts of daydreams are not likely to be a part of fully conscious thought. Dreams are playgrounds for the interaction of many events, and this free flow of thought often leads to new concepts.

## *The Importance of Diversion*

Because problem solving and creativity are helped by mental rest, diversion must be a part of the striving for answers to research problems. Despite their great aid to new ideas, playful actions are rarely part of the routine. If one is always uptight, tensing for the breakthrough solution, the free rein of diverse thought needed to shape new concepts is absent. For example, my conscious thought process peaks when I am rested and relaxed yet wide awake. One cup of coffee can help this process. This state of mind is often in concert with outbursts of inspiration seeming to come from nonconscious thought. One should use whatever method induces a state of free-flowing thought: Relaxation can do it for some, whereas others may require more unique methods.

It may seem that incubation is incompatible with leader guidance, but an all-consuming focus on a specific problem can actually be counterproductive. Incubation is helped when people have more than one task. Most people make breakthroughs only after projects related to the specific problem have been stopped.[14] It is crucial, however, that people's schedules not be so cluttered as to preclude a focus on primary work, to have the time to follow unique thoughts, or to explore novel events.

These cautions stress the stubborn nature of incubation and the benefit of having more than one task. Stopping a project for a short time after intense effort can help. Perhaps the nonconscious mind is always shuffling knowledge patterns until a unique fit makes complex data clear. And the solution is found.

## Stimulation

Certain kinds of mental action can be helpful in rousing new ideas. Figure 7 shows three general kinds of mental actions that can help in the stimulation step of discovery: basic research, external stimuli, and thought processes.

## Stimulation

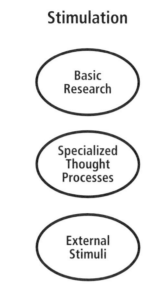

*Figure 7.* **Mental actions for stimulation**

## *Basic Research*

Although many data support the belief that technology greatly improves productivity, the effect of basic research has been ignored. Because of the long delay between the gaining of basic knowledge and new products and processes, the beneficial results from basic research are often unseen. It is simply logic that basic knowledge must precede inventions. In many mature firms, strategic basic research can lead to new growth.

Basic research is crucial to the gaining of new knowledge. But many people don't realize that basic research can also be a potent source of new thought patterns. It can pique resolve, and it can arouse the thought process to be more acute. The greater the resolve and depth of effort, the greater the chances of contact with the creativity center of the brain.

Research can be divided into four categories: empirical, literature, dialectical, and hypothetical. Empirical research is the primary way of gaining new knowledge. It is what is meant most often by the word "research" in science. It involves inductive thinking and is the knowledge gained through experiment and observation. The best way to gain a better understanding of an event is to probe responses resulting from a range of tests. Although an event can never be explained fully by this process, inductive logic is the most common view of the process of science.

When one becomes deeply involved in a research project, reading pertinent papers has greater meaning. The process of relating knowledge patterns can rouse strong feelings. Intense literature research, perhaps, is the most cost-effective method for knowledge gain. Beyond the goals of new knowledge and problem solution, the process of literature research and research in general can arouse a ferment that can increase the chances for discovery.

Dialectical research, that is, exchange about research problems with a broad range of people, can provide a wealth of new concepts and approaches. It can arouse better thoughts than those that come from an isolated group. The final goal of such research is to find the best aspects of a large group of thoughts and then from these produce a new idea of greater merit than any simple blend of those ideas. Because of proprietary information and budget restraints on travel, this type of research often is not done. The full value of exchange is known only to those who take part. It is one of the best ways to give new vigor to research projects.

Hypothetical research, or modeling, is the process of building concepts to explain events. Concepts designed to explain events provide a guide for experimental work. All hypotheses that seem to have truth should be explored in order to prevent a too-narrow research focus from stifling the most creative concepts.

All four types of research must be a part of research programs. Although this statement is agreed on in spirit, it often is not carried out in practice. This is most often true in industry, where demands are so urgent that only the most likely concept receives support. The novel approach is found most often through the study of all likely concepts.

Anomalies are the sources of serendipity in research. What at first seems inconsistent or contradictory may turn out to be a major chance for new knowledge. Research is started by a focus. Unless this focus can be kept clearly in sight and success seems likely, research should be controlled by anomalies.

Science is driven largely by anomalies; technology is driven by the market. People tend to become fixed on what their employer is asking, while being aloof to what the serendipity of research is pleading with them to study. The employer pays their salary, but anomaly is more often the source of new products.

## Specialized Thought Processes

When I left school many years ago to work in industry, I was steeped with the seeming magic of the scientific method. I am still highly impressed with its great power. My belief now is changed, knowing that new ideas often stem from intuition and inspiration—not just from induction and deduction. Sticking to the restraints of logic, therefore, may stifle free thought and block the novel. Although great progress has been made via the scientific method, unconventional thought is the most likely path to creativity. The concept is then made formal and constrained by logic.

Science projects are carried out linearly and logically. The process of discovery, however, is as varied as are the natures of people. By indirect means, false ideas have led to some major findings. Archimedes discovered how to measure the volume of an irregular body by surprise. Sir Alexander Fleming found penicillin after a tear from his eye accidentally dropped into a culture. Thomas Edison's inventions came from wrong theories of electricity. No matter how wrong thinking may be, if it leads to new methods, useful discovery is often the result.

The importance of the unconventional is strengthened by George Bernard Shaw's poignant syllogism: "The reasonable man adapts himself to the world; the unreasonable one persists in adapting the world to himself. Therefore, all progress depends on the unreasonable man."[15]

However, unconventional thought is not the only source for ideas. Although unconventional thought greatly increases the odds, many novel ideas seem to come from conventional thought. For example, Charles Darwin used analogous thought creatively. For his theory of evolution, Darwin used the idea of gradualism, gained from his training in geology. Edison used the concept of the cylinder as analogy in many of his inventions.[16]

These kinds of thought probably were not the only ones involved in any of these cases. Unconventional thought was likely involved more than historical studies indicate. It seems, however, that with intense effort, broad knowledge, and the right social conditions, conventional thinking can lead to new concepts. These methods of thinking are treated in detail in Chapter II.

## *External Stimuli*

The interaction of a new person with a research group having other views often leads to discovery. When James Watson went to work at the Cavendish Laboratory of Cambridge University, he brought a unique knowledge of genetics. Francis Crick, then at the laboratory, was using X-ray diffraction and creating math tools for the study of large helical molecules. The interaction between these patterns of knowledge led Watson and Crick to find the double-helix structure of DNA.

Another way to promote external stimuli is to present and publish research papers. In this case, researchers must interpret data with great care so that they will not be embarrassed in front of their peers. The presentation and publishing of research papers offers an opportunity for exchange outside the safety and bias of one's own lab. These actions can also enhance image and knowledge interaction and can help establish global contacts.

23

# Illumination

I have taken liberty in how I define an AHA!—the illumination stage of the creativity model. It may be only a new fragment of knowledge or, in the best sense, a new order derived from a unique blend of ideas or patterns of knowledge. An AHA! may be the discovery of something that has always been around, such as nuclear energy, or it may be the creation of something that has never been before, such as a Shakespearean play.

Serendipity, an unplanned result, is also an AHA! Because it is the common result of careful research, it is not strictly dumb luck. Horace Walpole coined the term serendipity in 1754. Reading the fairy tale of "The Three Princes of Serendip," Walpole noted that "as their highnesses traveled, they were always making discoveries by accident and sagacity, of things they were not in quest of." [17]

As stressed throughout this book, discovery is achieved by searching many paths. Finding a new path, right or wrong, can become useful to discovery. It is a common key to novel concepts.

Albert Einstein relied on the elegance of theory to lead him to the most novel and useful concepts. His superb brain greatly aided his success. Not everyone could derive theories as elegant as relativity. Creating elegant theory, without supporting empirical evidence, was a new method of doing science and now has great merit in scientific fields that are poor in data. Learning new ways of doing science should be a goal of all who create.

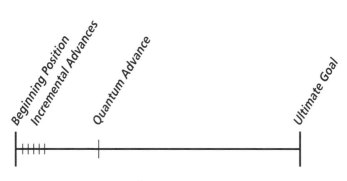

*Figure 8. The nature of research goals*

Although creators strive to make major discoveries, small advances are the rule (see Figure 8). Small advances are almost always the result of attempts to achieve greater goals.

The Japanese are geniuses in making incremental advances, and they make great improvements in profitability by this means.[18] Cultural in origin, incremental advances represent a method that departs from what has been a custom in the West. Miniaturization is one result: bonsai trees, mini cassette recorders, and hand-held video cameras.

If only the thrill of discovery could be taught, science would advance at a much faster pace. Perhaps then, business leaders of the world would have a better feeling for the needs of creative people. Sadly, profound feeling for the methods of discovery comes only after much practice. For the good of all, the nature and abstract quality of discovery needs to be researched and widely communicated.

# II.

## MODES OF THINKING
## THAT LEAD TO DISCOVERY

T HREE TYPES OF THINKING can be useful in the search for discovery: common sense, or natural; conventional, or scientific; and unconventional. Common sense is based on daily events and like science is founded largely on inductive and deductive logic. Unlike science, common sense does not have controlled experiment and consensus within the science body for voiding wrong beliefs. An extreme case of common sense is the gambler's fallacy, or the belief that an event is more likely because it is past due. Common sense often must be displaced by unexpected ways of nature.

Conventional thinking as I have classified it is the common method of science. The basic thinking of science includes deductive, inductive, and abductive reasoning. Unconventional thinking includes less common methods that often lead to the novel. For example, a common method involves thinking without the restraints of logic, as in daydreams. The study of an event should begin with conventional thinking, from which a major knowledge

platform can be built. When one departs from this platform, novel thoughts are often the result.

# Conventional Thinking

The most common ways of seeking knowledge are
through deductive, inductive, and abductive logic. These
are the classic thought processes used in the scientific
method. Figure 9 shows other methods often used in
science.

    The man who opened this Pandora's box of ways of
thinking was a pre-Socratic Greek, Thales of Miletus. He
made a unique statement in about 600 B.C. saying that
"the mysteries of the universe are governed by laws that
can be discovered in thought."[19] From Thales's thought

| | |
|---|---|
| **Deductive** | Conclusion follows from premises |
| **Inductive** | Reasoning from observation and experiment |
| **Rationalism and Empiricism** | Rationalism embodies deductive reasoning; empiricism embodies inductive reasoning |
| **Abductive** | Adoption of a hypothesis |
| **Socratic Method** | Dialectic or the art of breaking an argument into its parts |
| **Paradigmatic** | Normal or revolutionary approach to science |
| | • Normal    Thinking within a prevailing paradigm |
| | • Revolutionary    Thinking in a new and different paradigm |
| **Analogical** | Use of a similar approach to problem solving |
| **Reductionism** | Study of a part as opposed to the whole |

*Figure 9.* ***Some conventional thought processes***

there followed an outbreak of activity that Bertrand Russell said was the most striking event of history.[20] Both philosophy and science evolved in this milieu that was ancient Greece.

## Deductive Thinking

Deductive thinking is the logic of argumentation. It is the process of starting from one or more beliefs from which we deduce other ideas. Called rationalism, it is a form of logic used in science and in daily affairs. The premises are thought self-evident and can be classified as universal or individual truths. Thus the process of science produces new knowledge derived from research. From these beliefs is derived a further belief: Research is the process of science.

## Inductive Thinking

Inductive thinking is seen as the logic of discovery in science. Like deductive thinking, it is used in both science and the daily routine. In science, however, controlled experiments are performed from which observations are made. This cycle may be done repeatedly until a useful answer is derived. Inductive thinking is the thought process of empiricism.

## Rationalism and Empiricism

In the two thousand years before the Renaissance, all areas of study were servile to the Church. Not only did science decay in the Roman world, but until the Renaissance, earthly events had little meaning in contrast to holy beliefs. Scripture, prayer, and faith in the teachings of the Church were believed to be the basis of truth. The deductive logic of Aristotle was adopted by the Church as the only valid form of argument.

In the thirteenth century, Roger Bacon pushed the idea of empiricism. He showed the need to support concepts by experiment and observation.[21] Not surprisingly, in pushing his belief, he roused the ire of the Church and spent fifteen years in prison. The religious grip on science lasted until the seventeenth century, when it was upset by Francis Bacon.

Looking for a method of thinking that would strengthen deductive logic, Bacon showed that to grasp nature one must begin with observed fact rather than with prejudice. The notion of induction was not new, though, as Aristotle had already used it. Bacon, however, was the first to state clearly the great need for a new logic. To break the iron grip of Aristotelian logic, Bacon was a man of great prestige with the social strength to enforce his beliefs.

George Johnson contended that much of "the history of ideas has been driven by a tension between rationalism and empiricism."[22] Rationalism is the belief that valid study must begin with self-evident truths from which nature's laws can be derived. This is the method of deductive logic.

Empiricists believe that what can be known must come by way of the senses and, therefore, must rely on inductive logic. In this view, our brains begin as a blank slate and remain blank until the advent of experience. This concept is held by a school known as logical empiricists. It is much more recent than rationalism. For greatest efficiency, scientists today recognize that there must be a close working relationship between rationalism and empiricism.

## *Abductive Thinking*

Although it had been believed that hypotheses were the result of either deduction or induction, C. S. Peirce conceived that neither view was true.[23] To account for such thinking, he proposed a new process, which he called abduction. The process is one of finding other hypotheses, which leads to the adoption of the most likely concept.

The truth of a hypothesis is decided by deduction, which is seeing if the hypothesis fits the facts. If the hypothesis is approved it is a matter of abduction. Hypotheses are never stable, and as new facts are gained new hypotheses may evolve.

One's percept of the world is built over a lifetime and is inscribed in a neural network in billions of cells throughout the brain. Only those percepts that fit our pattern of beliefs are apt to be acquired. Given the long-term effort required to construct the neural network, it is clear why people strongly defend an idea, an ideology, or a faith. We cling to many of our ideas because they give us the illusion of control and they may solve some of our problems.

Reconstruction of the neural net into a new picture of the world may come, if at all, with great effort. The best defense against this enemy of knowledge is to be intensely aware of the problem and to give high credence to the process of hypothesizing. Create all likely hypotheses, and test each with great care.

Abductive thinking in science is a primary source of creativity. Being the vectors of progress and, therefore, springboards for action, hypotheses are required for science to proceed. When a new fragment of knowledge is acquired, it should never be viewed simply as rote memory but as discovery. The question should always be asked, What impact does this new data have on my body of knowledge? Is a new approach needed? In the interest of finding the most useful idea, one should feel bound to study all likely ways of problem solving.

## *Socratic Method*

First used by Zeno and later by Socrates and Plato, dialectic thinking, the art of breaking a subject into its parts by question and answer, is of great importance to science. Science groups and journals developed during the scientific revolution in seventeenth-century Europe. These developments greatly aided the dialectic and modern science.[24] In contrast to dialectic, eristic was practiced by the Sophists of ancient Greece. Today it is the art of those lawyers and politicians who twist thoughts to produce incorrect but desired conclusions. Defense attorneys must rationalize and make the worst actions of their clients appear acceptable or untrue. Politicians sometimes deny inappropriate actions, or try to make them appear respectable. As Bertrand Russell explained, "those who practice eristic are out to win, and those who practice dialectic are out to discover the truth."[25]

The dialectic can be with other people, with oneself, or with the past. In his adult life, Einstein had an exchange with his childhood questions of nature, a common way of achieving breakthroughs.[26] As a youth, he puzzled over the behavior of the point of a compass and the thought experiment of riding on a light beam. With the sophistication of his adult knowledge of physics, he was able to solve problems relating to these questions.

## Paradigmatic Thinking

According to Thomas Kuhn, science is a process that takes place within a paradigm.[27] Defined by Marc De Mey, a paradigm in science is "the whole set of shared beliefs and skills which shape the expectations of a community of scientists and establish a common directionality in their activities."[28] In forming his concept about revolution structure, Kuhn was perplexed that a man of Aristotle's brilliance could be so wrong about nature.[29] By viewing ancient Greece in its time, Kuhn then saw that Aristotle's view was common sense. It was common sense to believe that bodies have spirits and those like air rise and those like earth fall.

From this idea, Kuhn saw that scientists work within a system derived from their culture—a vision that shapes the way we see things, guides the thought processes, and dictates the vector of research. The precise nature of the paradigm is controlled by the most influential scientists. As science is about common belief within the body, selling of ideas becomes crucial. Therefore, some people see science as a social construct.

Despite allowing scientists to know what research to pursue, a paradigm in science has a basic problem: It dictates research vector. It is a tunnel vision that limits what can be seen. Such concepts are reshaped by paradigm shifts, which come about with great pain. Sometimes, the death of a major scientist is required before a shift can occur.

Newtonian gravitation, Darwinian evolution, Einstein's theory of relativity, and the Watson-Crick double-helix model of DNA are some classic examples of paradigm shifts in modern science. They shattered concepts and scorned common sense. The old guard agreed to these new concepts, if at all, with great pain. If discoveries depart from common wisdom, they are often opposed.

The major work done in science is classified as normal. This amounts largely to gaining new data within a paradigm. It is the final stage of discovery. In contrast, major shifts in theory are a result of those who persist to explain anomalies from a fresh view. In a sense, discovery picks the finders. Discovery has a clear liking for those people who have freedom of thought, who are intense in the effort applied, and who are primed with knowledge.

## *Analogy*

Creative work starts with what is known and what has been done before. An invention may begin with the memory of a similar method that could be used to solve a problem. Such a method is a link with the past, but it becomes novel by being interacted with new knowledge in unique and useful ways. For example, the Wright brothers used birds as a model for wing-warping.

Although thinking by analogy is used frequently and is classified here as conventional, it is a common aspect of novel thinking as well. Those who produce novel works of great moment do so because they possess high levels of knowledge (analogues and associations) and skill, and are led by intuition, logic, and stubborn will.

## Reductionism

The scientific revolution, which occurred in the latter part of the Renaissance, changed our view of the world. An important idea that arose during this time was that problems could be made easier to solve by breaking them into their parts—a method called reductionism. John Stuart Mill called this "the method of detail." Its growth was in concert with mechanistic philosophy. Problems that seemed too difficult to solve by the old method were solved by studying the parts. The method of detail had a major effect on the scientific revolution, new machines, and the growth of industry.[30]

Feelings toward reductionism relate to the science involved. In the social sciences, it cannot address emergent complexity. In data-rich fields, such as physics and chemistry, it is the most successful route for learning.

## Unconventional Thinking

Conventional thinking is important to science and technology, but it also promotes the status quo. Unconventional thought is a major source for new concepts. Some unconventional methods of thinking are shown in Figure 10.

| | |
|---|---|
| **Holistic** | Interaction of more than one knowledge pattern |
| **Pyramidal** | Stubborn approach to problem solving |
| **Elegant Theory** | May preclude empiricism |
| **Fuzzy Logic** | Multivalent logic, true, false, and indeterminate |
| **Lateral** | Use of the best path to problem solving |
| **Knowledge Based** | Finding best path through breadth of related knowledge patterns |
| **Heuristic Search** | Establishing rules of thumb for problem solving |
| **Janusian** | Showing opposites to be true at the same time |
| **Visual** | Mental imagery |
| **Homospatial** | Synthesis of merging percepts |
| **Metaphorical** | Relating ideas and defining limits |
| **Hemispherical** | Thinking by brain asymmetry |

*Figure 10.  **Some unconventional thought processes***

## *Holism*

Holism is in stark contrast to reductionism and entails the study of all the parts of a problem together. As reasoned by the German philosopher Hegel, progress of a concept must end, which is the Absolute. This Hegel believed to be the only truth from which it follows that no portion of the whole has meaning.[31] Even found among the pre-Socratics, this concept of holism occurs throughout history. In Einstein's general relativity ($E = mc^2$), neither the energy nor the mass of a system can be clearly defined at any point. It is, therefore, a holistic concept.

Fritjof Capra's systems approach to nature promoted the holistic concept—the essential relation of all of nature.[32] Such a concept stems from the strange conduct of subatomic matter that cannot be viewed as lone parts. Quantum theory has shown that subatomic particles are probability patterns, which perforce are related throughout nature. This concept also applies to the consciousness of human beings. For example, the electron does not have properties free of our minds. If we ask a wave question, we will get a wave answer. If we ask a particle question, we will get a particle answer. These concepts, however, have limits in use.

It is a helpful and often needed reduction to study a lone event and to think of all else to be without meaning. Reduction is a process that furthers problem solution, which may be out of reach by any other method. This warping of truth permits us to gain at least a working idea of how nature functions.

The level of reduction in science, however, may reach a point at which coherent results are no longer produced. Although the holistic approach cannot always be achieved, it should be used more often than it is. Probing lone events without concern for how they relate to other things can make some research seem trivial.

Society could not function without some level of reductionism, however. For example, the field of medicine is so vast that we could not obtain correct care without the knowledge of specialists. Further, the need for specialists becomes greater as science becomes more complex. The holistic approach, however, offers the best chance for new concepts. It is needed to support the growing and novel needs of the world.

## Pyramidal Thinking

Pyramidal thinking, a term that I created, is as much a state of mind as it is a way of thinking. Although the term is new, the idea is not. It is an aspect of science by which hypotheses are created until the process peaks at a novel solution. The key to this kind of thinking is positivism, asking oneself how to solve the problem if failure can mean dire results. For example, if a new product fits a clear need of industry but is too costly, a major effort is then made to reduce costs. It is always easier to explain why a system will not work than to find a way to make it work.

Many people throughout a company become involved in the innovative process, and all of them can be important to the program's success. Some of these people may not have the needed drive to put forth the required effort. Such weak links can destroy the efforts of others. Worthwhile innovation is rarely easy, and its success requires an intense effort. It is the technology leader's job to impart a pyramidal, positive feeling in the technical staff. But all of management should instill the perseverance necessary to the company-wide task of innovation. The danger exists, however, that a problem may be probed beyond a reasonable limit, or that a new technology may render yours unneeded. Determining the project end is a judgment call, and the wisdom of knowing when to quit evolves with knowledge and practice.

I have brought in the term "pyramidal" to adjust the idea of conventional thinking to creativity. No kind of thinking leads to creativity without intense effort. Thus the greater the effort, the greater the chance for novel results to come from conventional thought. Enter pyramidal thinking, which often leads to new concepts. This method changes conventional thinking in science into the unconventional. In the extreme this concept evokes a new meaning: Lack of enough effort results in only conventional thinking; major effort effects novel thought.

## Elegant Theory

Although induction is a primary process of science, another method usurps this process and shows that the ways of science are not fixed. Elegance, clearness, and neatness of the fit can enable a theory to prevail, even without empirical evidence. Galileo supported Copernicus's heliocentric theory of movement of planets despite the absence of empirical proof. Such proof did not surface until more than two hundred years after Galileo's death. He was so convinced of the theory that he was willing to risk the wrath of the Inquisition.

Einstein's general theory of relativity also had wide support many years before empirical evidence was obtained. In Einstein's view, the logic and simple clearness of a theory had greater meaning than did experimental evidence. He was in concert with the ancient Greeks in the belief that novel concepts are needed in order to grasp nature. Despite the great utility of elegance, it does not become true science until after empirical justification— essential to reliable knowledge.

## Fuzzy Logic

Although fuzzy logic is still developing, it seems to provide a new and useful way of thinking about science and technology. Fuzzy thinking is grayness, multivalent logic—true, false, and vague. Bivalent logic—true or false—had its start with Aristotle and is still used by science today. In fuzzy logic, light is both wave and particle, but in bivalent logic it is either a wave or a particle, not both. Matter obeys Einstein's laws of general relativity and Newtonian mechanics for large objects. For subatomic particles the laws of quantum theory apply. The area between these two extremes is unclear and fuzzy. In Aristotelian logic, bivalency is stated as A or not A; the grass is green or not green. Fuzzy logic is A and not A, where the grass is both green and not green. Paradoxes are often both true and not true; for example, a Cretan says that all Cretans are liars. Only fuzzy logic can solve this paradox.

Fuzzy logic may cause a major change in the ways of science and technology. Gray logic must be used to describe a gray world. This approach avoids the roadblocks of paradox. Perhaps just as important, fuzzy logic would effect a major change in thought processes that may lead to discoveries now out of reach.

## Lateral Thinking

Edward de Bono pointed out that lateral thinkers explore all of the ways of looking at a problem: common, devious, and otherwise.[33] This attitude is in opposition to that of vertical thinkers, who accept what seems to be the best method and then neglect all others.

A visual example of these concepts is the nine-dot problem shown in Figure 11. The problem is to connect all nine dots with four line segments without lifting your pencil from the paper. The solution is shown in Figure 12, and as described by Robert Sternberg, most people cannot solve the problem.[34] Although nothing in the stated problem hints of border constraints, an assumption is made that the lines cannot be drawn outside the framework outlined by the outer dots. Prior experience can impose a mental block to thinking in new and novel ways. Not only does this case show the need to clearly define the problem, it shows the need to approach problems from many viewpoints.

Jerry Conrath showed how the nine-dot problem can be solved with three lines or even one line.[35] Using three lines, start one at the extreme left of the upper left dot. Then go through the middle of the left middle dot and through the extreme right of the lower left dot. This line must be extended for a very long distance. Return

*Figure 11. The nine-dot problem*

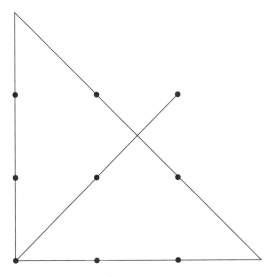

*Figure 12. The nine-dot solution*

through the middle row of dots, again extending this second line a long distance, and then return with the third line.

With one line, a paint brush can be drawn through all nine dots with one swish. Another method involves cutting the paper and lining up all of the dots. These methods embody the thought processes of the lateral thinker. De Bono said, "There is no sudden conversion from a belief in the omnipotence of vertical thinking. Lateral thinking is a matter of awareness and practice—not revelation." [36]

## Knowledge-Based Thinking

Another aspect of lateral thinking is knowledge-based thinking. In opposition to this approach is object-centered thinking. An example of the latter is the car industry's past mind-set on large cars instead of small energy-efficient cars. Or to make an advance in lighting, the knowledge-based approach can entail the most energy-efficient method of making light. The object-centered approach, in contrast, is confined to better energy-efficiency of the incandescent light bulb.

## Heuristic Search

Problem solving can be viewed as a search within a metaphorical space. Algorithms provide a method for investigating all the paths in a problem space and for finding the correct path. Problems in areas such as checkers and chess are so complex and the space so large that neither algorithms nor lateral thinking may be helpful. For example, in a typical game of chess a total of 60 moves might be involved with the potential of 30 alternate moves for each of the 60 moves. Astronomic in size, the total number of paths for the game is $30^{60}$, which is called a combinatorial explosion.[37] Here the fastest computer could not explore all moves. Although human players can look ahead no more than three or four moves, a grand master can play better than any computer program. It seems only a matter of time, however, until computers will defeat grand masters, even without time limits.

In these areas of huge problem space, the heuristic search method is used. Only a few moves that seem most likely to provide a solution are considered. General rules gained by experience enable experts to make moves that will enhance their position. For example, a move might be made to help control the center of the board. Such a move is better than one that does not.

Heuristic search is feasible as long as the best possible solution is not required. By virtue of the development of expertise, the extent of the search for finding a reasonable solution can be reduced to an acceptable level. If problem solution requires finding the best path, heuristic search is futile and brute force is the only choice. The heuristic approach gives great credence to the importance of knowledge and experience. In this way, not only is the approach made more simple in chess, it does so in all areas of thinking.

## Janusian Thinking

Rothenberg found that Janusian thinking is common to many people who create.[38] Named after Janus, the Roman god of beginnings, who is shown with one head and two bearded faces, one facing left and one facing right, this kind of thinking occurs early in the creative process. It is a way of thinking to show that two opposing ideas can be true at the same time. Oxymorons, such as bittersweet or violent quiescence, and fuzzy logic with respect to paradox are Janusian concepts. Such dual meaning is basic to the conflicts found in poetry and prose. As opposed to common wisdom, we can have it both ways, perhaps more. Stubborn probing of things that oppose each other may help solve otherwise puzzling problems.

An example of Janusian thinking was provided in the sixth century B.C. by the Chinese philosopher Lao-Tsu: "We put 30 spokes together to make a wheel, but it is on the space where there is nothing that the usefulness of the wheel depends. We turn the clay to make a vessel, but it is on the space where there is nothing that the usefulness of the vessel depends. We pierce doors and windows to make a house, but it is on the space where there is nothing that the usefulness of the house depends. Therefore, just as we take advantage of what is, we must recognize the usefulness of what is not." [39] Poignantly shown is the usefulness of unconventional, Janusian thought. Awareness and persistent probing of opposites may lead to problem solutions that could not be derived by conventional methods.

## Visual, Spatial, Metaphorical, and Hemispherical Thinking

Visual thinking for problem solving is most useful where shapes, forms, or patterns occur. [40] Our conscious and our nonconscious minds are concerned with mental images more than any other form of thought. What we see is what we are most apt to believe. [41] Visual thinking is useful in most problem solving and in creativity. For example, although they can speak, blind children find it difficult to impossible to solve problems. In contrast, deaf children, without verbal use, can use their vision to solve problems.

In most people, visual thinking occurs in the right half of the brain. Varied thought processes occur in the two hemispheres in ways that seem to shed some light on the source of novel thinking. If one hemisphere of the brain is damaged or removed in childhood, the other half takes over without loss of function. High specialization precludes such an offset in adults. [42]

As a rule the left hemisphere controls language, logic, order, math, and certain motor skills. The right hemisphere is better at spatial functions: visual thinking, face and pattern recognition, and proportion. The better the working relationship between the two brain halves, the more creative one is apt to be.

Rothenberg described a kind of visual thinking that he called homospatial.[43] He found that this kind of thinking often occurs in the latter part of the creative process. It entails thinking of two or more objects in the same visual space that then evolves into a new form. For example, parts of a landscape may be merged and interacted with human faces, written words, and so on. Helen Keller summed up the impact of vision and visual thinking in one sweeping statement: "Use your eyes as if tomorrow you will have been stricken blind."[44]

# III.

## Making Creativity and Discovery a Reality in Company Operations

T O INVENT, ONE IS SEEKING, along with discovery, an existential high. When I was a Marine paratrooper during World War II, I would feel such a high after a safe jump—a profound feeling of being alive. If you achieve discovery, even though minor, you will feel a similar high. At least for that moment, life can seem a paradise. Such feelings strengthen the desire to discover.

During discovery, an algorithmic path often is taken first; sequence and order are prime. Then a new approach, often without the restraints of logic, takes one along many paths in time and space. This is the approach that most often leads to the realm of novel ideas.

In addition to technical methods of approaching novel concepts, methods of leading are also crucial. In industry, novel concepts have little meaning unless they are transformed into profit. Technical and management methods are discussed in this chapter. Commercialization to profitability also is considered briefly.

## Stimuli for Creativity

The creative process begins with knowledge gain and ideally goes through preparation, incubation, stimulation, illumination, and verification. New ideas often result from using the scientific method along with breadth and depth of knowledge, the great power of the dialectic, holism, and the mystique of novel thinking. The following suggestions can help increase the chances for novel ideas:

1.  Be deeply immersed in your profession.

2.  Carry out diverse research projects and maintain worldwide exchange.

3.  Have a profound hope of causing a ripple in the wisdom of the world.

4.  Free your mind of thought constraints.

5.  Find the strength to defy the conventional.

Table 2, pages 50–51, presents a detailed approach to achieving creativity. The steps shown follow the model in Figure 1. They are designed to preclude the strictures imposed by thinking only with the conventional logic of science.

New ideas for products can be generated by conducting technological market surveys, as described in Chapter I, and by doing research in accord with the stimuli for creativity. In pursuing new product ideas, the stages shown below should be followed generally:

Stage I:   This stage requires broad applied knowledge and entails thorough probing of new knowledge to derive new research, product

upgrades, new product concepts, or
process concepts.

Stage II:   This stage entails using applied research,
market research, process research, and
costing in designing the new product
concept to achieve profit.

These approaches—technological market surveys,
stimuli for creativity, and the two stages for new product
study—can be thought of as parts of a rough algorithm for
achieving novel results. There is no way to know all the
avenues that people follow to achieve their creative goals.
Following these general approaches with free rein, however, is a useful guideline. The first two steps in the algorithm shown below apply to knowledge gain and idea
generation; the two stages for new product study also
apply to idea generation and to the final part of new
product development.

| Technological market surveys | + | Research via stimuli for creativity | + | Two stages for new product study | = | New products |
|---|---|---|---|---|---|---|

Talented people are crucial for innovation. They
must be convinced of their mission to find new knowledge
and to change it into profit. This dual approach is also
crucial. Some research people consider the process of commercialization to be mundane. Others become so involved
in their basic efforts that they lose contact with the need to
apply their findings. Without a dual quest to discover and
apply, useful knowledge may never get into the hands of
would-be entrepreneurs.

| Creativity Model Stage | Steps Helpful to Creativity |
|---|---|
| Knowledge Gain | • Choose a work setting that has a keen and broad ranging intellectual spirit. |
| | • As an ongoing process, seek a vast breadth of knowledge, at least in the sciences and the arts. Carry out diverse research projects and look for linkages that create new knowledge. |
| | • Focus on the most basic points of knowledge patterns, as opposed to the minute details. |
| | • Through the process of knowledge gain and publication, develop the strength to defy convention. |
| | • Do not be afraid to seek intellectual unconventionality. |
| Preparation | • Choose those problems of study for which you have basic drive. Choose those issues that are not fads, that may be thought too puzzling by others, and that are anomalies. |
| | • Create your own approach to the first stages of problem solving. Give special thought to steps that will transcend common thinking. |
| | • Make certain that the needed basic science is known before launching into targeted research. |
| | • Question all beliefs. |
| Incubation | • Carry out several tasks and more than one research project. |
| | • Take respites from the most puzzling problems to allow incubation to proceed. Respite is achieved partly by having other tasks and partly by taking a rest from puzzling problems. |
| Stimulation | • Allow anomaly to drive your research. |
| | • Practice holism. |
| | • In the approach to problems, do not rely solely on expert knowledge. Strive to become the Leonardo da Vinci of your field, or at least the most broadly knowing person in the company. Look for connections with other areas of science. |
| | • Seek hands-on knowing in your approach to problem solving. For new product work, conduct technological market surveys. |

- To avoid mind-sets, test all likely concepts. Be firm in your effort to find the best idea. Strive for elegant theory.
- Do not focus on an idea until all others with merit are given thought.
- Follow intuition and curiosity in all aspects of problems under study.
- Allow and promote humor in your research efforts.
- Promote diversity by exchange with global contacts, by presenting papers at professional meetings, and by traveling in order to experience diverse events.
- To assist the search for truth, attempt both to confirm and to falsify theory.
- Always view new knowledge in the sense of discovery— probe the effect it may have on your knowledge. What other questions does new knowledge pose? What other research should be carried out? How can this knowledge be used to improve products or create new ones?
- Be aware of the power of the scientific method, but also know its limits and the need to transcend common science thinking.
- Seek a broad range of thought methods, including verbal, visual, and spatial thought.
- Tease the thought process into peak action by looking for conflict; think of things that are alike, that are not alike, of things that are opposed, and of "what ifs." Create paradox.
- Be aware of the uncertainty of knowledge, not only to avoid mind-sets but to be more alert to flaws in concepts and to accept change.
- Always be aware of the huge potential for discovery.

Illumination
- Prepare in-house reports with the same effort applied to manuscripts.
- Be thorough in writing papers to publish and to present at technical meetings. Strive for the best.

*Table 2.   A working approach to creativity*

The raw truth is that there is nothing easy about the discovery process. It requires hard work and constant knowledge gain in a highly interactive milieu. Although the work is hard, if one begins to feel the highs of even minor success, the process can become nearly perfect pleasure.

## Management of Discovery

The primary tenet of this book—that innovation is the most crucial goal of technology—is based on industry experience that the most successful firms continually find novel and useful ideas. Given this tenet, the three most important goals of a technology group are (a) discovery, (b) new product ideas, and (c) help in the translation of new ideas into profit.

Eleven tenets of discovery management summarize the most useful methods for achieving these goals:

1. Promote a highly interactive knowledge-based system through lab structure.

2. Enforce a judicious balance between time used for innovation and time used for other tasks.

3. Promote the study of anomalies, aid the success of projects, and dare all people to be the best in their field.

4. Promote a mood of pristine honesty and a freedom to express ideas.

5. Support the needs of incubation—more than one task and intense study followed by a respite from the problem in question.

6.  Promote diverse strategic research to address the weakest links in the understanding of critical problems.

7.  Promote an air of wide-ranging thought, using some thought methods outside the bounds of the routine.

8.  Assert the value of knowledge exchange both in and outside the lab.

9.  Reward all idea growth, and make certain that the best ideas are tested.

10. Promote intrinsic drive (pursuit of new knowledge for the enjoyment of solving the puzzle), and help people to control their future.

11. Sell to management the conviction that all people taking part in discovery must be honored for the process to flourish.

To ensure the best chances for successful discovery and innovation, continuously communicate and instill all of these tenets among the company's technical and research staff.

## Verification and Commercialization

If verification and commercialization are added to Figure 1, the system is transformed into a scheme for innovation (Figure 13). In industry, verification and commercialization are synonymous. By using the tenets, the stimuli in Table 2, the two stages for discovery in this chapter, and the methods for new product ideas (Chapter I), the system

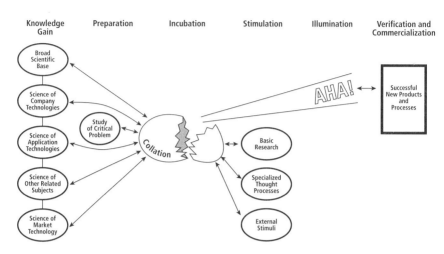

*Figure 13.  A schematic for innovation*

can be enhanced. Then the path to improve long-term company strength can lead to success.

The novel idea must be shown to be useful through innovation and widespread use. Until then, it is of little value. This process is often a long and difficult one, and it may require more effort than the discovery. In technology, such a process changes new concepts into profit.

Changing new concepts into profit may be the weakest area of industry. This step is crucial to the support of research, and it should be carried out with the same intense effort applied to discovery. Although research people cannot be the sole movers of the profit picture, they should offer as much assistance as is needed to transform ideas into company gain.

In the company in which I worked, successful innovation came only where sponsorship was carried out diligently by the president. Because it is commonly the only way in which adequate cooperation can be achieved, authority across divisional lines is important to the introduction of new concepts. Sponsorship of great strength is critical in any company. Without it, the self-interests of each division often come first. The ideal situation is one in which the interests of all divisions could have greater commonality.

The support of industrial research depends on commercial success. And commercial successes are largely up to technical and nontechnical management's understanding of the discovery process. For new technologies to be commercial successes, inventions must be of high quality. This does not mean that every detail must be documented before commercialization or that risks should not be taken. Early introduction of new technologies may be necessary to establish a competitive position. High-quality inventions make successful commercialization possible. A profound understanding of the discovery process can enhance invention quality.

To minimize the obstacles that are inadvertently placed in the path of innovation, management, from the president to the technology manager, should develop an empathy for the needs and mechanisms of discovery and the process of innovation. Under such conditions, companies can be competitive. And, at the best, they can operate from a position of scientific, technologic, and economic dominance.

# IV.

# THE TECHNICALLY CREATIVE ENTERPRISE

NOVEL IDEAS CAN BE thought of as treasures, hidden in a clutter of ignorance, mind-sets, and false beliefs. To see beyond this clutter and to discover the treasures involves hard work, desire, and the will to change ideas until the problems in question are resolved. Our primary hope for future wealth rests with our educational system, government policy, the methods used by industry to strive for growth, and a growing knowledge of how to invent.

Education must help make the public aware of the nature of science. Students should be taught to think on their own and to deal with profound ideas. This should always be done with the love of knowledge. If invention is to be a major part of our future, it will come about because people are firmly convinced of its value. A climate for invention must prevail.

Our focus must be on anomaly as a primary route to progress, with targeted research supported by underlying science. Those who control the funding of research must promote, by careful choice, a variety of methods for problem solving.

That some people oppose technology is understandable. Witness abuses such as smog, strip-mining, and pesticide residues. There is no shortage of problems. It would be naïve, however, to assume that fewer problems would have arisen without technology. Problems develop whether we do nothing or are highly involved in technological change. If one reflects on the huge strides in medicine and living standards, the credit balance surely favors technology. Life would be shorter, harder, and boring without it. If we could not strive for answers, revel in the process and the answer, feel the flow of energy that comes from novel ideas, or have the hope of progress, life could lose meaning. *Homo sapiens* would not have survived without discovery.

## Industrial Creativity

Strategic basic research is crucial to the discovery of new ideas. Because high returns are required over the short-term, however, people often strive for ideas that will give the largest and quickest payoff, even when needed basic knowledge is lacking. Because the benefits may not be fully known for years, basic research has been stopped in many companies. The delay period for useful results is longer than these companies are willing to wait. This paradox, seeking short-term high returns without crucial knowledge, reduces returns. Much can be learned from the way things are done in the best companies. Prime cases are Merck and 3M, where innovation drives success.

Late in my career, my former company was acquired by a large corporation. Sometime after then, our operating committee was informed by a group vice president that he and the other corporate managers were not concerned about the long-term. In this context, ten years down the road did not have meaning. Growth of margin in the short-term was the primary goal. We on the operating committee were appalled, but not surprised, at such a statement. Our feelings were mixed, wanting to be loyal yet sad with the short-term focus. The hard work of innovation seemed to lose meaning and purpose.

Being more stubborn than realistic, some of us secretly maintained the long-term track, as best we could. We did this even though upper management maintained a focus on the short-term. This paradox is common, with innovation required in the short-term, despite the need of long-term effort to achieve goals. Such conflicts can lead to greatly reduced growth.

The United States can learn three lessons from Japan and Germany: (a) long-term investments are important, (b) educating people is crucial, and (c) do not neglect a focus on small change.[45] In those countries, technologists are often in the top ranks, rather than lawyers and finance people, as in the United States.

Ketteringham and Nayak have described six guidelines for aiding innovations, based on their study of twelve major breakthroughs in the past twenty years:[46]

1.   Decide to invest a certain amount of money in long-term research.

2.  Select those people for the long-term work who are most likely to make breakthroughs.

3.  Back the projects these people choose.

4.  Make sure that the projects draw upon the organization's strengths and are directed to a problem the market cares about.

5.  Don't rely on market research.

6.  Make sure that management joins the team.

These guidelines have been designed for all and can be most helpful for large corporations. The people chosen to work on the new ideas should have breadth and depth of experience and a strong desire to carry out their projects. Team members must interact with other in-house functions and with customers that may profit from their project. If market knowledge is conveyed to the team only by market research reports, a great deal can be lost in visualizing new products.

I continue to be astounded by the fact that many technology managers are required by common practice to devote most of their time to detailed paperwork and frequent meetings. They are then chastised for not discovering new ideas for profit. If both the short-term and the long-term are to be addressed, the primary concern must be discovery, incremental change, and the translation of ideas into profit. 80 percent or more of their time should be devoted to these tasks. Morale is addressed best by success in the primary goals of discovery, not by paperwork and nondiscovery types of management.

George Heilmeier, Industrial Research Medalist for 1993, has identified the traits of the best companies: "They have leaders who know the business. They have close contact with the market at all levels. They have a very low incidence of NIH, the 'not-invented-here' syndrome. They minimize formal internal communication and rely heavily on informal or ad hoc communication. They have strong personal incentive systems. Their people are not afraid of failure; they take intelligent risks and try more things."[47]

What would the ideal environment and the ideal company for innovation look like? First, let me review three crucial measures for success:

1.  High-talent research people with an intense desire to invent and to convert new ideas into profit. The company is willing to go the extra mile to hire the best people. To hold these people and to foster new products, strategic basic research has support.

2.  A research group with knowledge of ways to create new product ideas that fit market needs. Research people have the dual mission of discovery and of changing new knowledge into new product ideas. They then help change new product ideas into profit.

3.  A company culture in concert with the current knowledge of ways to discover, to the process of innovation, and to the need for company-wide cooperation. Companies that wish to be innova-

tive must first have an insight into how to discover. Their design of control systems must fit the subtle needs of creativity.

## The Ideal Environment for Innovation

In the ideal environment for innovation, creativity and discovery are honored. The public has knowledge of the power and limits of science and technology. Both are held in high esteem, and many of the brightest students seek careers in these areas. Learning is valued by all and is geared to promote profound thinking.

Government and industry work in concert to control and prevent bad effects from technology. While technology is valued as a major factor in the support of growth and jobs, social welfare is also respected. Innovative firms thrive in this environment. They are honored for what they invent and for their restraint from actions having harmful effects. Incentives are offered by the government to promote long-term company goals and to develop future technologies. Merger-mania and its bad effects on the long-term are deterred.

To address the high cost of equipment and leading-edge research, the government devises ways for collaborative research between firms. Wall Street, convinced of the great value of long-term research, does not punish lack of growth in short-term profits if there is ample evidence of sound long-term planning. Authorities that fund research change their focus from projects that will give mundane results to those most apt to surprise.

# The Ideal Company for Innovation

The ideal firm's leaders are not only technically knowing but have a profound knowledge of all aspects of the firm. Technical knowing means an in-depth knowledge of how discoveries are made and a working knowledge of the technologies involved. New process and new product goals are backed strongly by all leaders. All members of the firm are given good reasons to help in both goals. Conflicts in goals are shunned, and innovation is viewed as a common goal. Through learning programs and on-site action, the basics of innovation are learned and used.

Business units within a large firm have their own technology groups in order to encourage creativity, which is often suppressed in large organizations. Firm goals are short-term only to the extent needed to guide current operations but are long-term otherwise. By careful concern for the long-term, the short-term becomes more profitable. All sections of the company are honored and held in high esteem. Although major innovation is an important goal, incremental improvement of products and processes is highly prized as well.

Many technical people are on the management team and help give the needed push for novel approaches to problems. The technology leader has a broad in-depth background and is familiar with the basic needs of all branches of the firm. He/she has had training in creative leadership and in human relations, works with all leaders, and cooperation throughout the company works for the success of all.

The technology leader knows that for success, the technology staff must attract the best scientists and engineers. To build an expert team, the firm is willing to go beyond the norm in pay and leading-edge research. The technology manager is geared to promote novel efforts and to support the change of ideas into profit. Paperwork and meetings are minimized. Having holistic duties, the research staff includes all of the parts in their work. These parts may include strategic research, new product ideas, improvements of current products, and help in turning new ideas into profit. Culturally diverse, the firm is not afraid of smart risks, has overcome the "not-invented-here" syndrome, and is willing to try many things.

With a background in discovery, the technology leader has learned from on-site study of systems used by the best firms. The tenets of discovery management are followed (see Chapter III). Using most, if not all, of the stimuli for creativity listed in Chapter III, the staff enhances its chances for success.

All firm leaders understand the need for gaining required basic science before doing targeted research. Market needs are studied by the technology leader and the technical staff. The research effort is guided by the strategic plan, by change in the market, and by the anomalies found in research projects.

Knowing that his/her success is tied to the success of the staff, the technology manager helps in the work of each. Major accomplishments are communicated throughout the firm. Novel concepts have been profitably commercialized, adding to the group's esteem and motivation. By using these methods, the group's esteem has been fixed through high profit results. The firm has gained respect throughout the industry and among customers, and this respect enlivens the company's innovation process.

The ideal environment for innovation may be a dream, but we can move toward that goal. In the meantime, however, we can create the ideal firm. It is my hope that the ideas described in this book can aid in that effort.

# REFERENCES

1. De Bono, Edward. *Serious Creativity: Using the Power of Lateral Thinking to Create New Ideas.* New York: Harper Business, 1992.

2. Root-Bernstein, Robert S. "Strategies of Research," *Research-Technology Management,* May–June, 1989, pp. 36–41.

3. Bloor, David. *Knowledge and Social Imagery.* Chicago: The University of Chicago Press, 1991.

4. Calvin, William, H. *The Ascent of Mind: Ice Age Climates and the Evolution of Intelligence.* New York: Bantam Books, 1991.

5. Edelman, Gerald, M. *Bright Air, Brilliant Fire: On the Matter of Mind.* New York: Basic Books, 1992.

6. Klivington, Kenneth. *The Science of Mind.* Cambridge: The MIT Press, 1989.

7. Johnson, George. *In the Palaces of the Memory: How We Build the Worlds Inside Our Heads.* New York: Vintage Books, 1992.

8. Maturana, Humberto R., and Francisco J. Varela. *The Tree of Knowledge: The Biological Roots of Human Understanding.* Boston: Shambala, 1992.

9. Rothenberg, Albert. *Creativity and Madness: New Findings and Old Stereotypes.* Baltimore: The Johns Hopkins University Press, 1990.

10. Russell, Bertrand. *Wisdom of the West*. London: Bloomsbury Books, 1989.

11. Adams, James, L. *Conceptual Blockbusting: A Guide to Better Ideas*. San Francisco: W. H. Freeman and Company, 1974.

12. Wolff, Michael. "To innovate faster, try the skunk works," *Research-Technology Management*, September–October, 1987, pp. 35–36.

13. Adams, James L. *The Care and Feeding of Ideas: A Guide to Encouraging Creativity*. Reading, Mass.: Addison-Wesley Publishing Company, Inc., 1986.

14. Root-Bernstein, Robert S. "Strategies of Research," *Research-Technology Management*, May–June, 1989, pp. 36–41.

15. Gardner, John W., and Francesca Gardner Reese, *Quotations of Wit and Wisdom: Know or Listen to Those Who Know*. W. W. Norton & Company, Inc., 1975.

16. Weisberg, Robert, W. *Creativity: Beyond the Myth of Genius*. New York: W. H. Freeman and Company, 1993.

17. Root-Bernstein, Robert S. *Discovering: Inventing and Solving Problems at the Frontiers of Scientific Knowledge*. Cambridge: Harvard University Press, 1989.

18. Goleman, Daniel, Paul Kaufman, and Michael Ray. *The Creative Spirit*. New York: Plume, 1993.

19. Van Doren, Charles. *A History of Knowledge: Past, Present, and Future*. New York: Carol Publishing Group, 1991.

20. Russell, Bertrand. *Wisdom of the West*. London: Bloomsbury Books, 1989.

21. Ibid.

22. Johnson, George. *In the Palaces of the Memory: How We Build the Worlds Inside Our Heads*. New York: Vintage Books, 1992.

23. Russell, Bertrand. *Wisdom of the West*. London: Bloomsbury Books, 1989.

24. Bauer, Henry, H. *Scientific Literacy and the Myth of the Scientific Method*. Urbana: University of Illinois Press, 1994.

25. Russell, Bertrand. *Wisdom of the West*. London: Bloomsbury Books, 1989.

26. Gardner, Howard. *Creating Minds: An Anatomy of Creativity Seen Through the Lives of Freud, Einstein, Picasso, Stravinsky, Eliot, Graham, and Gandhi*. New York: Basic Books, 1993.

27. Kuhn, Thomas S. *The Structure of Scientific Revolutions*. Chicago: The University of Chicago Press, 1970.

28. De Mey, Marc. *The Cognitive Paradigm*. Chicago: The University of Chicago Press, 1992.

29. Kuhn, Thomas S. *The Structure of Scientific Revolutions*. Chicago: The University of Chicago Press, 1970.

30. Pacey, Arnold, *The Maze of Ingenuity: Ideas and Idealism in the Development of Technology*. Cambridge: The MIT Press, 1992.

31. Russell, Bertrand. *Wisdom of the West*. London: Bloomsbury Books, 1989.

32. Capra, Fritjof. *The Turning Point: Science, Society, and the Rising Culture*. Toronto: Bantam Books, 1982.

33. De Bono, Edward. *New Think: The Use of Lateral Thinking in the Generation of New Ideas*. New York: Basic Books, 1968.

34. Sternberg, Robert J. *The Triarchic Mind: A New Theory of Human Intelligence*. New York: Viking, 1988.

35. Conrath, Jerry. "The Imagination Harvest: Training People to Solve Problems Creatively," *Supervisory Management,* September, 1985, pp. 6–10.

36. De Bono, Edward. *New Think: The Use of Lateral Thinking in the Generation of New Ideas*. New York: Basic Books, 1968.

37. Holyoak, Keith, J. "Problem Solving" in *Thinking: An Invitation to Cognitive Science,* edited by Daniel N. Osherson and Edward E. Smith. Cambridge: The MIT Press, 1990, pp. 117–46.

38. Rothenberg, Albert. *Creativity and Madness: New Findings and Old Stereotypes*. Baltimore: The Johns Hopkins University Press, 1990.

39. Gardner, John W., and Francesca Gardner Reese, *Quotations of Wit and Wisdom: Know or Listen to Those Who Know*. W. W. Norton & Company, Inc., 1975.

40. Adams, James, L. *Conceptual Blockbusting: A Guide to Better Ideas.* San Francisco: W. H. Freeman and Company, 1974.

41. Harth, Eric. *The Creative Loop: How the Brain Makes a Mind.* Reading, Mass.: Addison-Wesley Publishing Company, 1993.

42. Restak, Richard. *The Brain.* Toronto: Bantam Books, 1984.

43. Rothenberg, Albert. *Creativity and Madness: New Findings and Old Stereotypes.* Baltimore: The Johns Hopkins University Press, 1990.

44. Goleman, Daniel, Paul Kaufman, and Michael Ray, *The Creative Spirit.* New York: Plume, 1993.

45. Chen, Katherine, T. "Contrasting Strategies Are Pursued by Big Three Economic Power Houses," *IEEE Spectrum,* October, 1990, pp. 76–78.

46. Wolff, Michael. "Fostering Breakthrough Innovations," *Research-Technology Management,* 1988, pp. 8–9.

47. Heilmeier, George. "Room for Whom at the Top? Promoting Technical Literacy in the Executive Suite," *Research-Technology Management,* 1993, pp. 27–32.

# FURTHER READING

This book presents a new way of looking at creativity and discovery in the sense of being holistic. Few if any references deal with the whole picture in the ways of current concepts of creativity and discovery, personal experience, technology management, and business approach. The following references may be useful if you wish to investigate certain aspects further.

Gardner, Howard. *Creating Minds: An Anatomy of Creativity Seen Through the Lives of Freud, Einstein, Picasso, Stravinski, Eliot, Graham, and Gandhi.* New York: Basic Books, 1991. An in-depth analysis of the circumstances leading to discovery in the lives of seven of history's most creative minds.

Root-Bernstein, Robert Scott. *Discovering: Inventing and Solving Problems at the Frontiers of Scientific Knowledge.* Cambridge: Harvard University Press, 1989. Probes the intricate methods used in many of the world's most important discoveries.

Tarnas, Richard. *The Passion of the Western Mind: Understanding the Ideas That Shaped Our World View.* New York: Ballantine Books, 1991. Presents an incisive account of the intellectual history of the West.

# About the Author

Dr. Bundy is a consultant and recognized authority in industrial mineralogy and in the management methods that produce discovery and creativity. After service in the Marine Paratroops and then the Fifth Marine Division in World War II, where he was wounded on Iwo Jima, he attended Indiana University and earned his Ph.D. in geology. He has held positions in the New Mexico Bureau of Mines, the Indiana Geological Survey, and Georgia Kaolin Company. He retired from Georgia Kaolin as vice president of technology. His research interests include mineral technology, surface chemistry, the rheology and functionality of kaolin, and the nature and implementation of discovery in science and technology.

Dr. Bundy is a former president of the Clay Minerals Society and a Fellow of TAPPI. He holds nine patents and has published widely in professional and trade journals.

Dr. Wayne M. Bundy, 3026 Chase Lane, Bloomington, IN 47401